The triplet Book for Violin

Part One   by Cassia Harvey

CHP267

©2015 by C. Harvey Publications® All Rights Reserved.

www.charveypublications.com - print books & free sheet music blog
www.learnstrings.com - downloadable books & chamber music

1

Left-Hand Warm-Up; D Major

Cassia Harvey

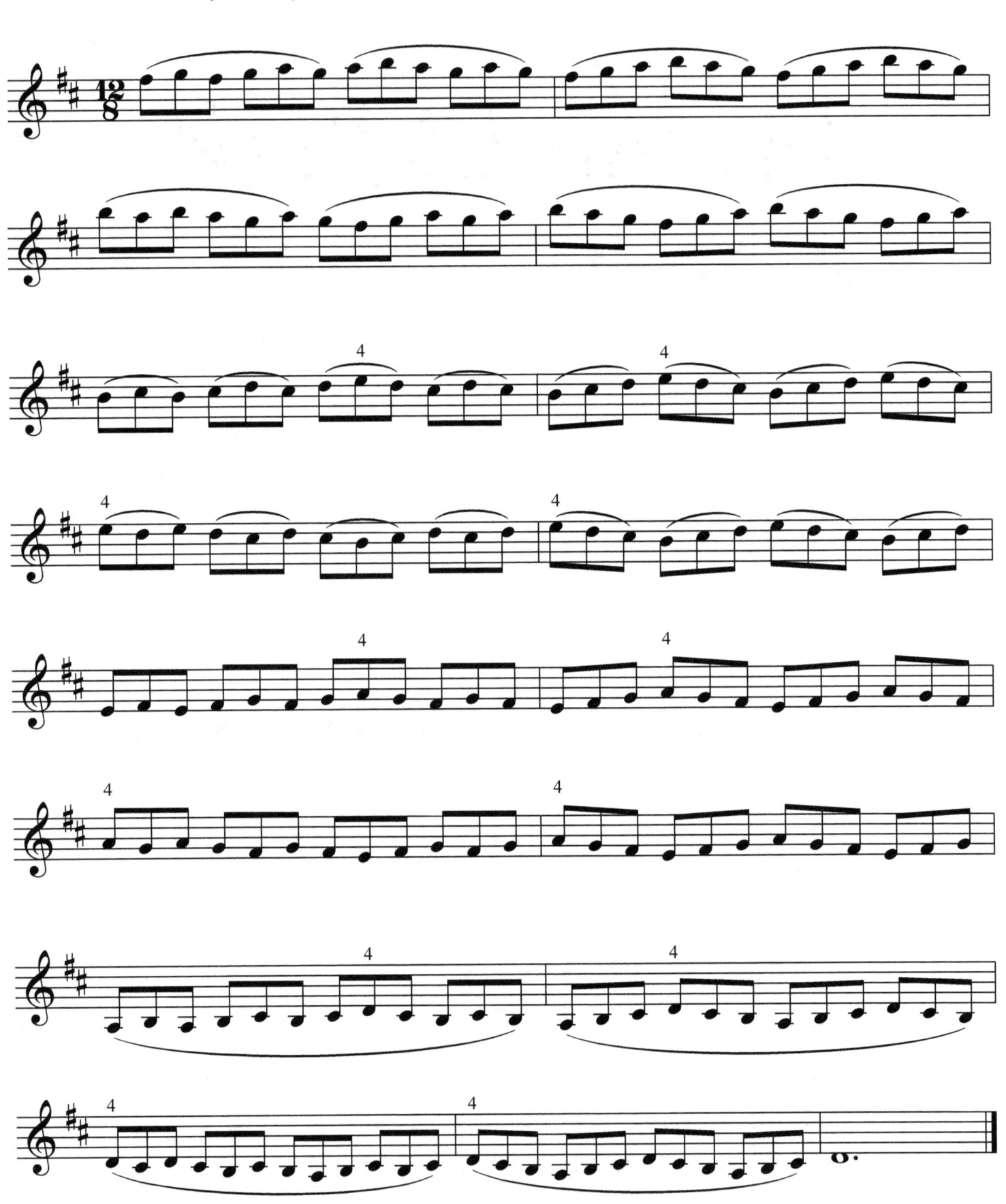

©2015 C. Harvey Publications All Rights Reserved.

3

String Crossing

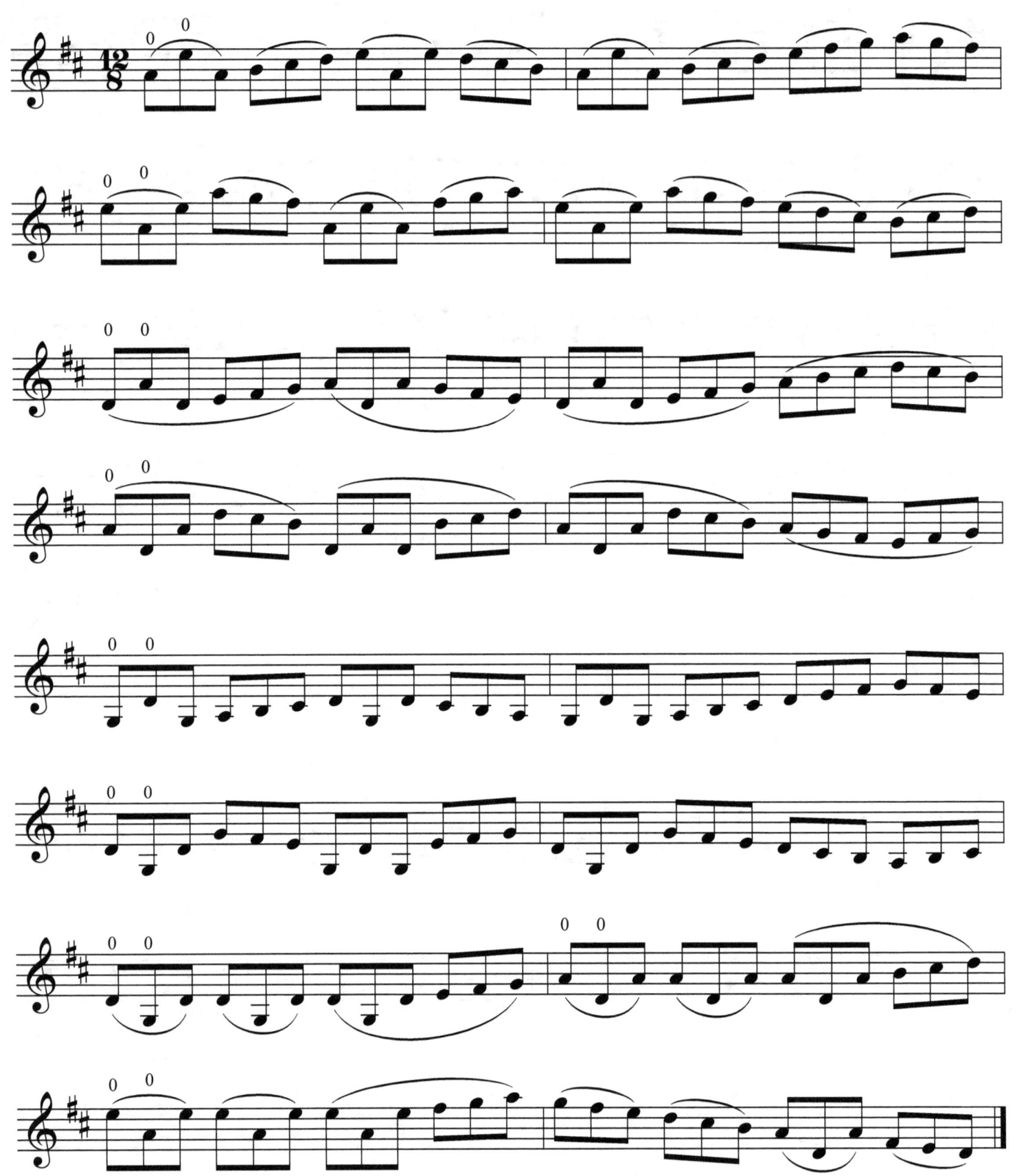

4

The Howlet and the Weazle — Trad., arr. Harvey

Neapolitan Threshers — Trad., arr. Harvey

5

Left-Hand Warm-Up

6

John James — Trad., arr. Harvey

Wicklow — Trad., arr. Harvey

7

String Crossing

8

Grenoside Sword Dance — Trad., arr. Harvey

The Mischevious Bee — Trad., arr. Harvey
(*Andante*)

9

Left-Hand Warm-Up

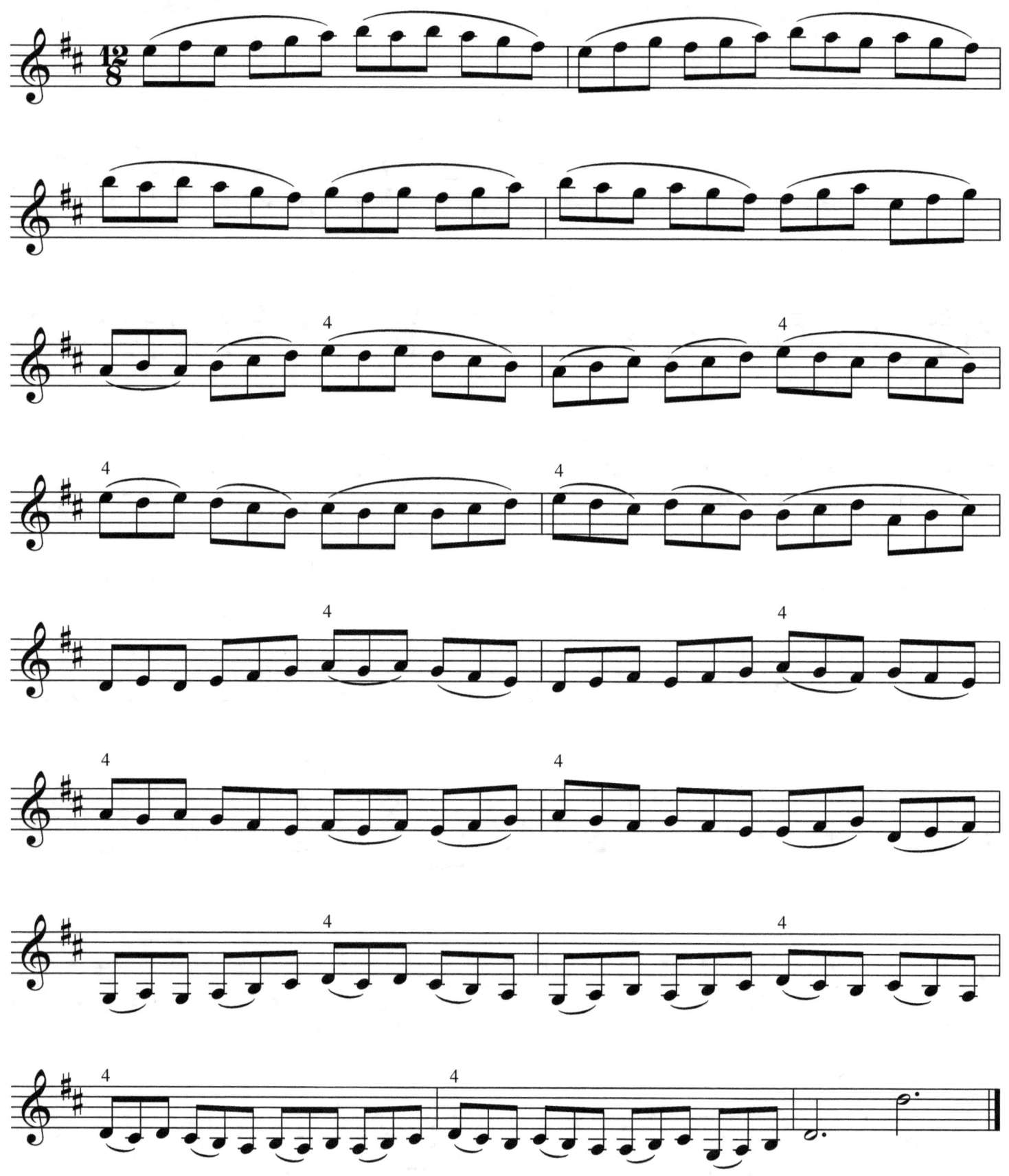

10

Gigue

Bast, arr. Harvey

11

String Crossing

12

Theme from Concerto Alla Rustica Vivaldi, arr. Harvey

13

Left-Hand Warm-Up: G Major

The Triplet Book for Violin, Part One

©2015 C. Harvey Publications All Rights Reserved.

15

String Crossing

16

Even and Odd

Trad., arr. Harvey

17

Left-Hand Warm-Up

18

The Sprig of Shillelah — Trad., arr. Harvey

Reel — Harvey

19

String Crossing

The Triplet Book for Violin, Part One

20

The Drum Major

Trad., arr. Harvey

Oh Dear, What Can the Matter Be

Trad., arr. Harvey

©2015 C. Harvey Publications All Rights Reserved.

21

Left-Hand Warm-Up

22

La Pastorale
Burgmuller, arr. Harvey

23

String Crossing

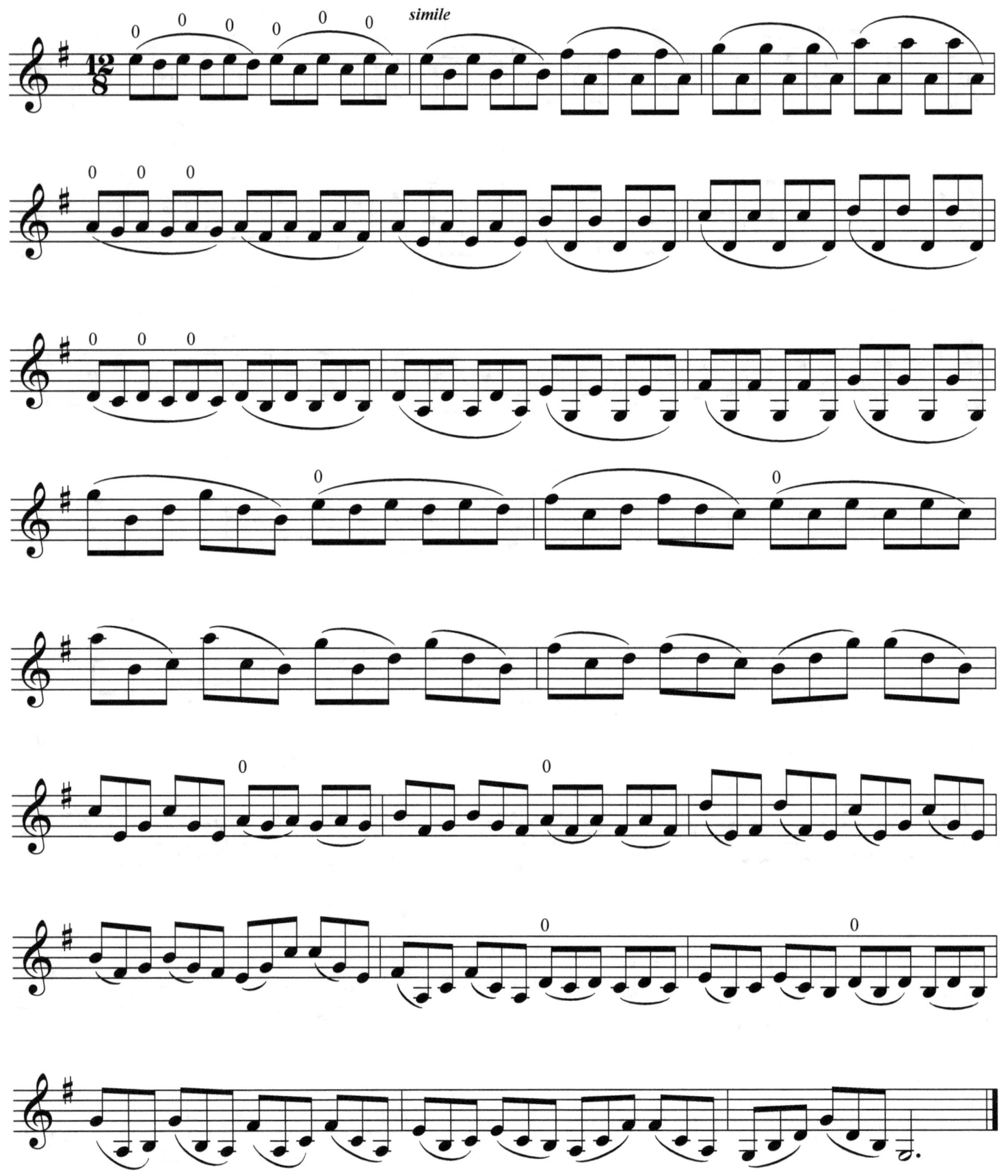

24

Study
Carl Fisher's Method, arr. Harvey

25

Left-Hand Warm-Up: C Major

The Triplet Book for Violin, Part One

26

Garry Owen
Trad., arr. Harvey

Gigue
Anon., arr. Harvey

©2015 C. Harvey Publications All Rights Reserved.

27

String Crossing

28

The Campbells are Coming — Trad., arr. Harvey

Haste to the Wedding! — Trad., arr. Harvey

29

Left-Hand Warm-Up

The Triplet Book for Violin, Part One

30

Allegro

Telemann, arr. Harvey

©2015 C. Harvey Publications All Rights Reserved.

31

String Crossing

The Triplet Book for Violin, Part One

32

Allegro from Brandenburg Concerto No. 6

Bach, arr. Harvey

©2015 C. Harvey Publications All Rights Reserved.

33

Groups of 6

The Triplet Book for Violin, Part One

34

Theme from Brandenburg Concerto No. 3

Bach, arr. Harvey

©2015 C. Harvey Publications All Rights Reserved.

35

Groups of 6

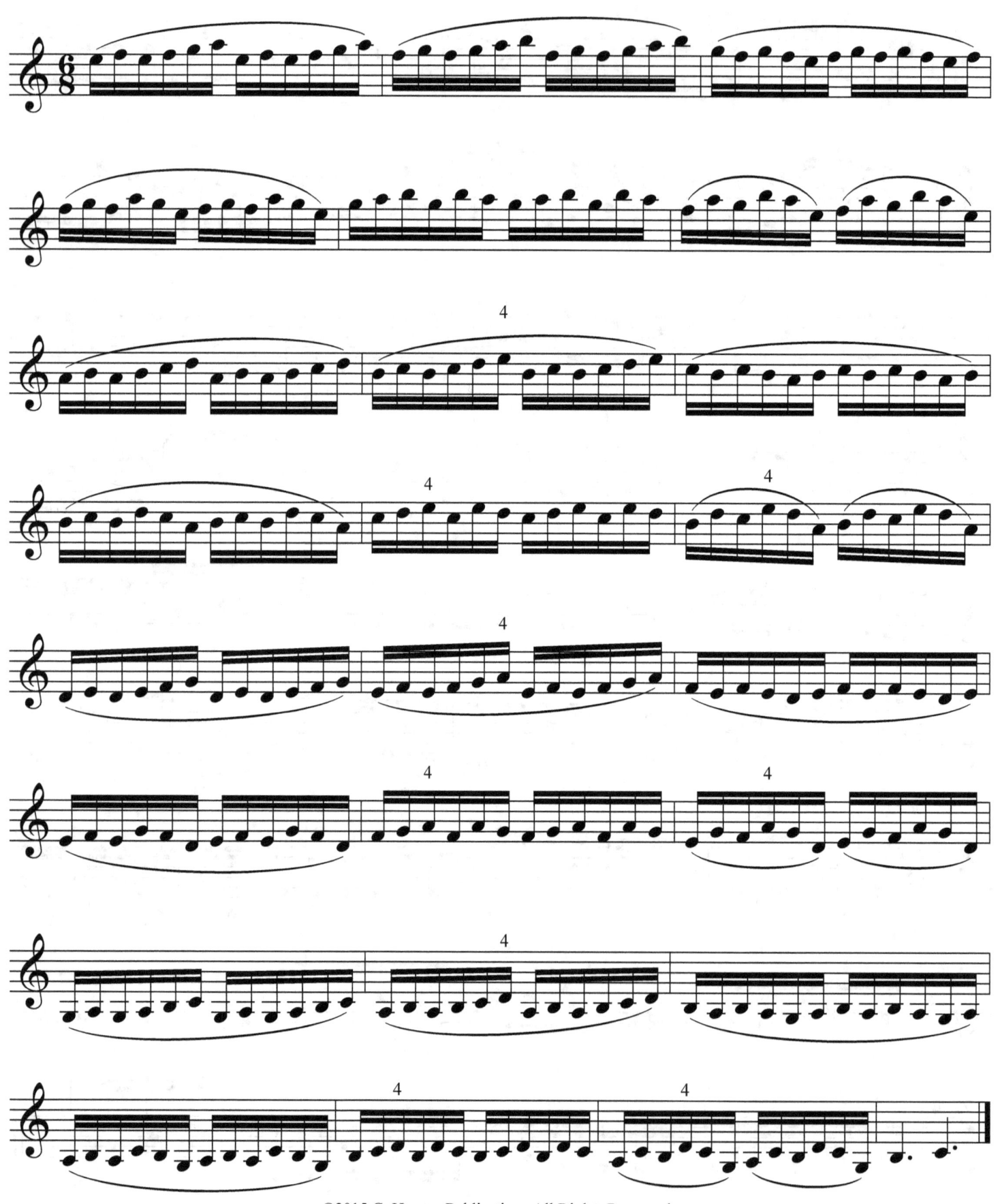

The Triplet Book for Violin, Part One

36

Albinia
Trad., arr. Harvey

©2015 C. Harvey Publications All Rights Reserved.

37

Groups of 6

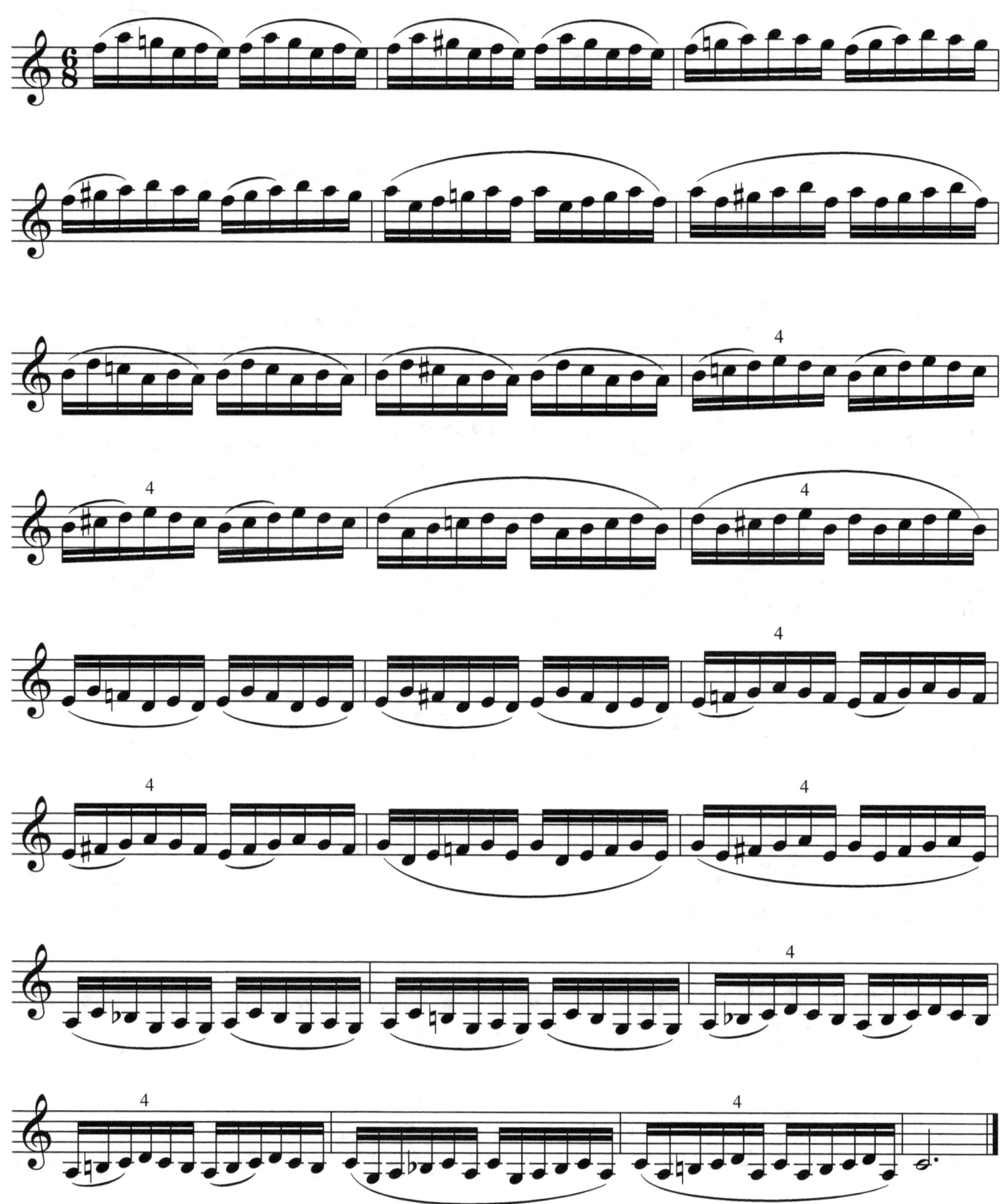

The Triplet Book for Violin, Part One

38

Lady Cholmolly's Waltz

Trad., arr. Harvey

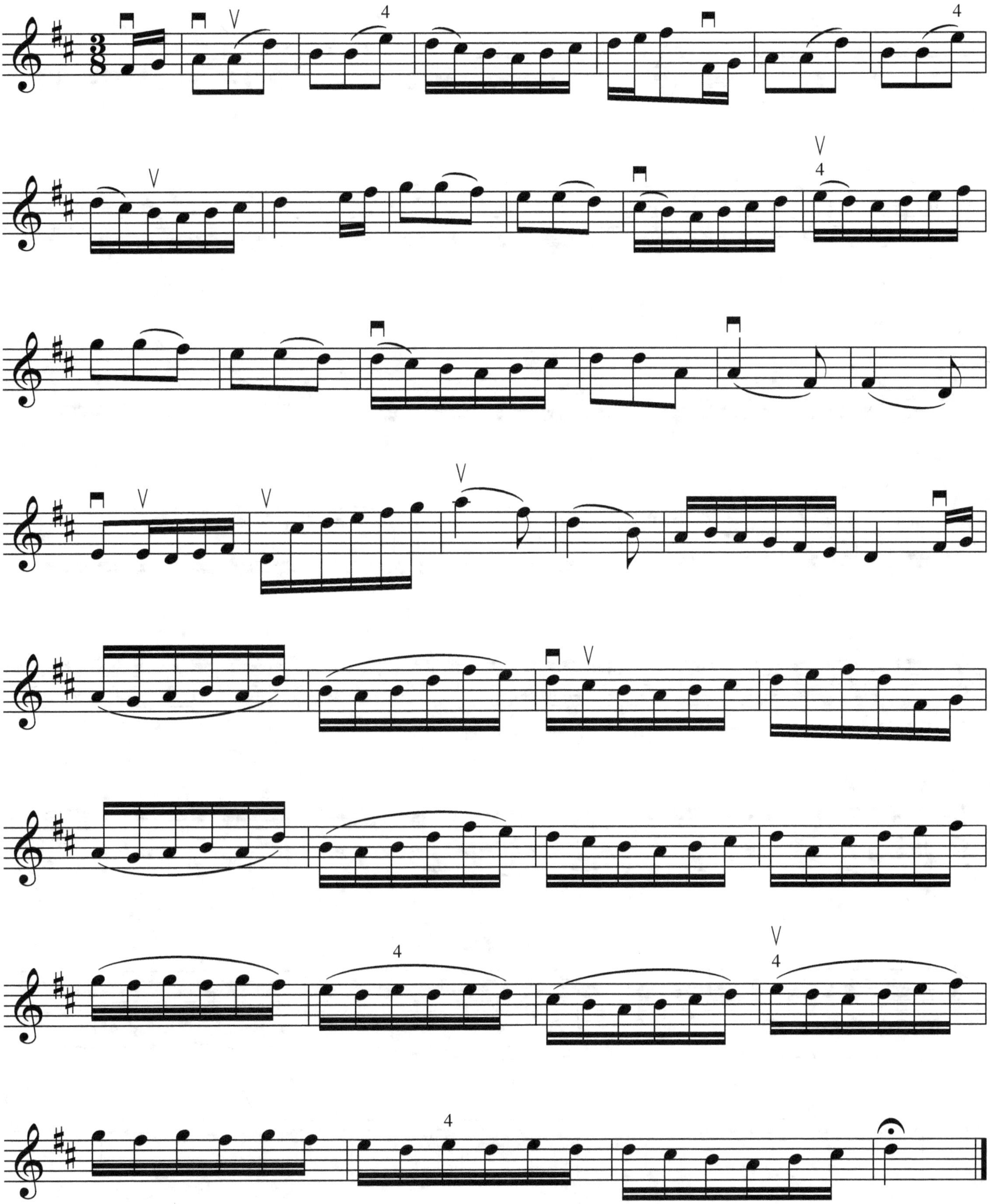

©2015 C. Harvey Publications All Rights Reserved.

40

The Triplet Book for Violin, Part One

39

Groups of 6

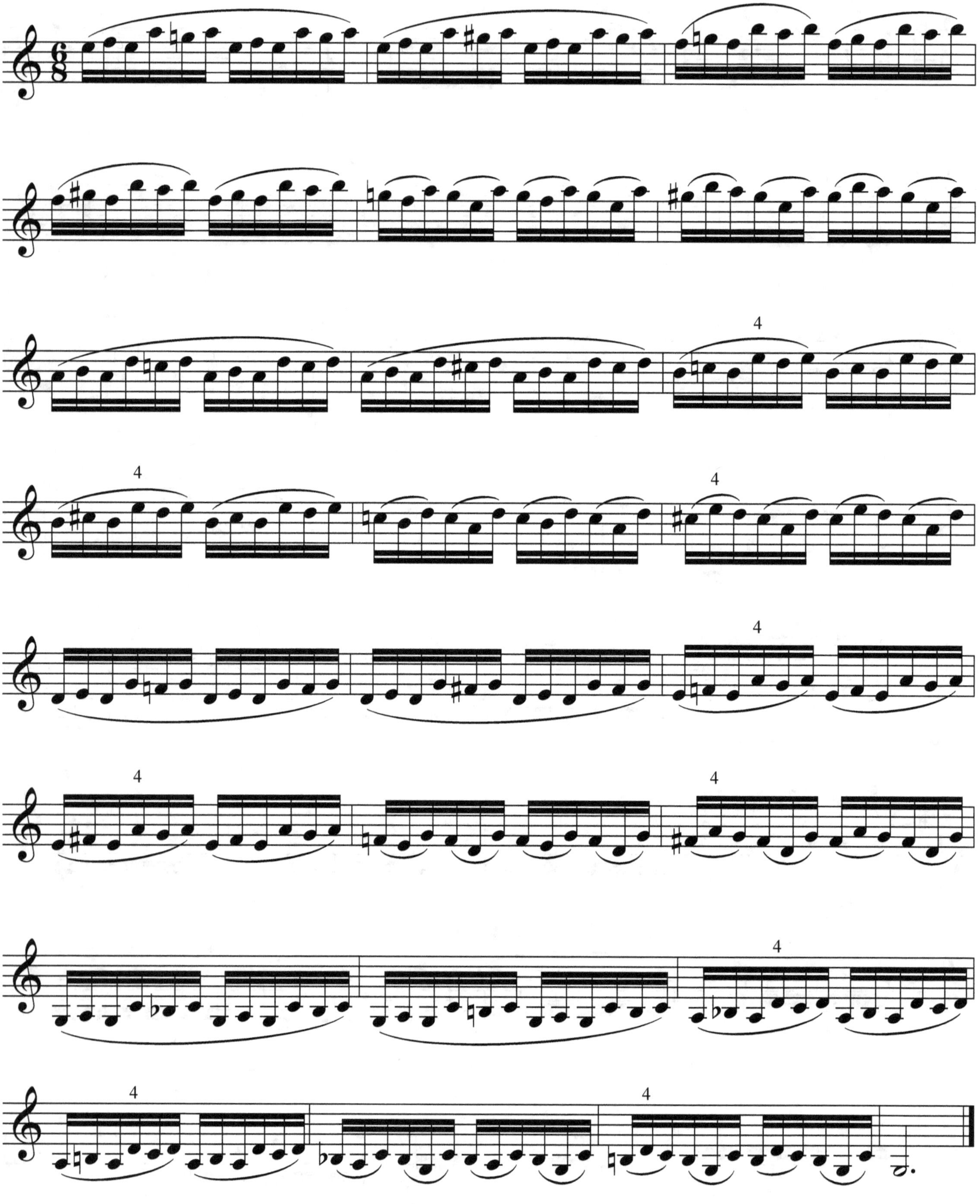

©2015 C. Harvey Publications All Rights Reserved.

40

Over the Water — Trad., arr. Harvey

41

Scale Bowings

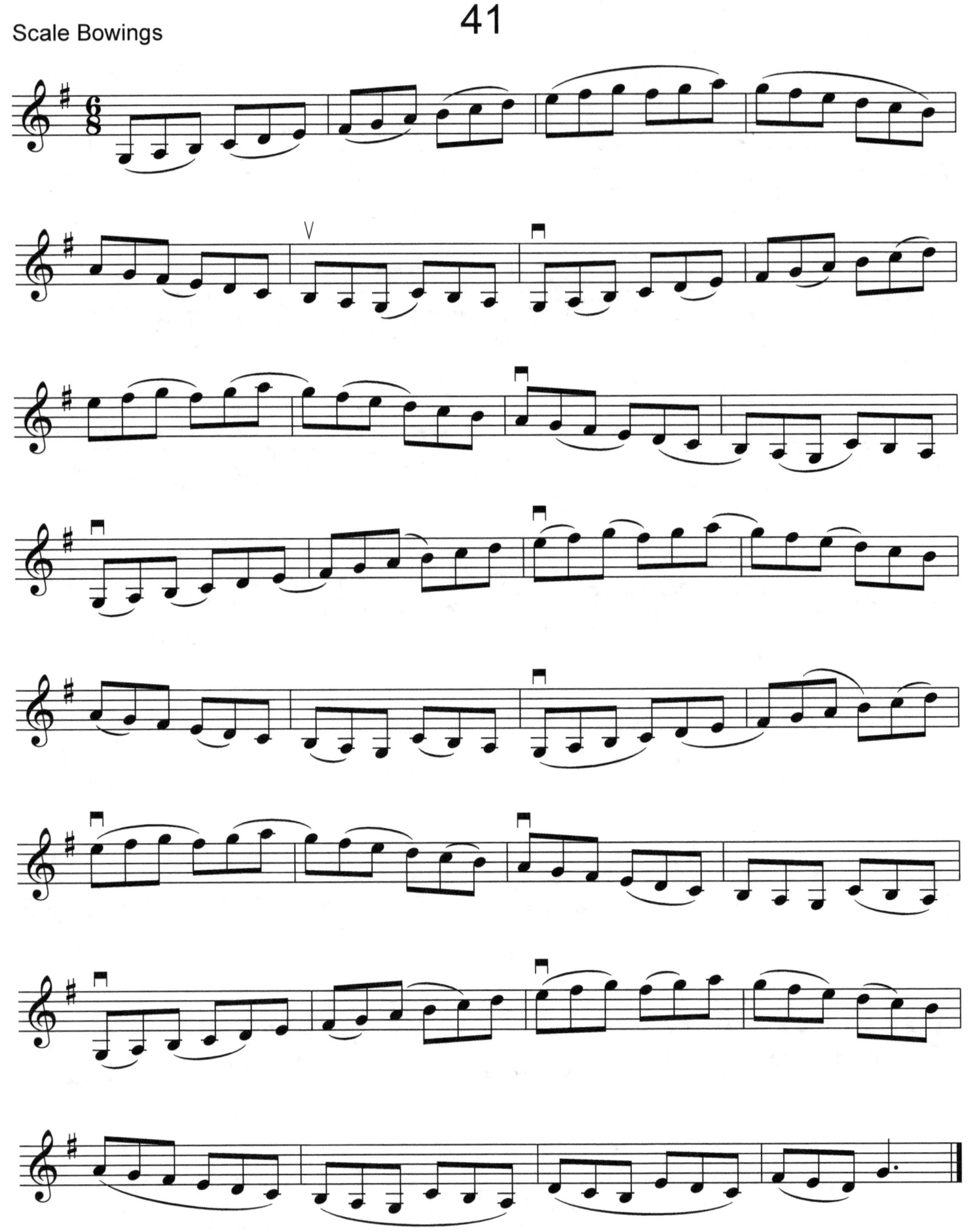

42

Gigue

Trad., arr. Harvey

44 — The Triplet Book for Violin, Part One

43

Scale Bowings

©2015 C. Harvey Publications All Rights Reserved.

45

Broken Thirds Bowings

The Triplet Book for Violin, Part One

46

Lord Palmerson's Favourite

Pringle, arr. Harvey

47

Arpeggio Bowings

48

Off She Goes — Trad., arr. Harvey

available from www.charveypublications.com: CHP254

Playing in C Major

Playing in Keys for Violin, Book One

Cassia Harvey

A key is like a language: every key contains certain notes and has certain rules.

The key of C major contains all the natural notes on the violin.

There are no sharps or flats in C major.

The notes in the key of C major are all of the notes in the C major scale,
so we will start by learning the notes in the C major scale that occur in first position.

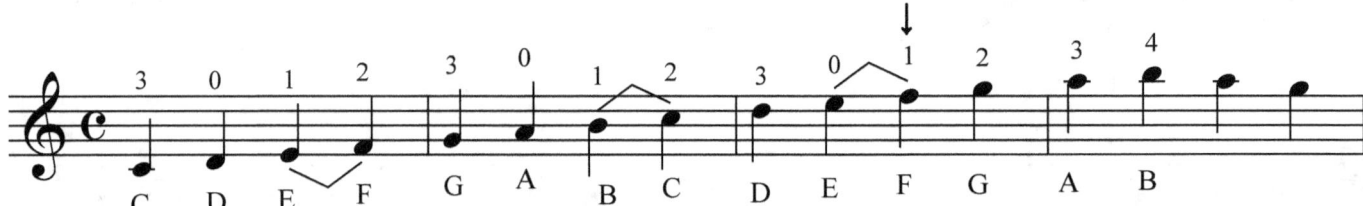

On the violin, the key of C major uses high 2nd finger on the G string
and low 2nd finger on the D, A, and E strings.
The key of C major also uses low 1st finger on the E string.

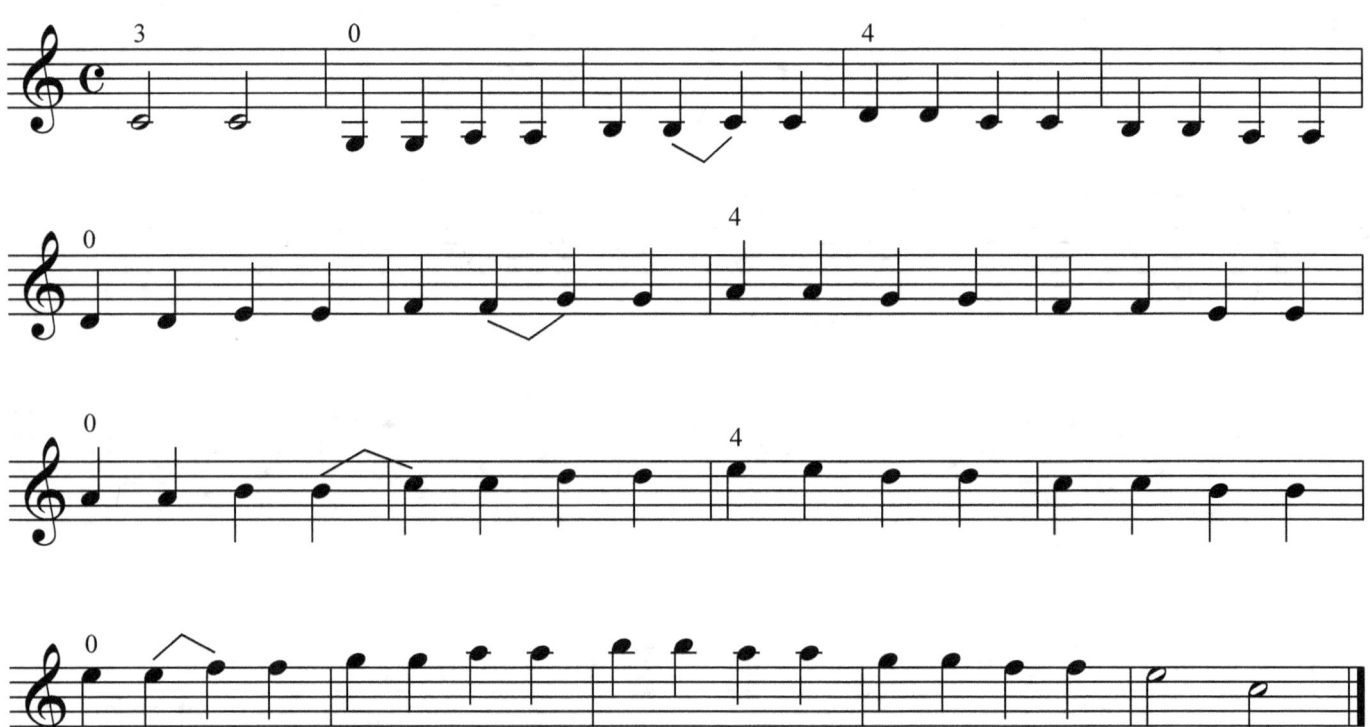

©2014 C. Harvey Publications All Rights Reserved.